OUR
SPACIOUS
SKIES

SUN, STORM AND STARS — A JOURNEY THROUGH DAY AND NIGHT IN THE HEARTLAND

Photography and text
Gary Lezak • Jen Winter • Vic Winter

KANSAS CITY STAR BOOKS

Published by Kansas City Star Books
1729 Grand Boulevard, Kansas City,
Missouri 64108

First Edition

Library of Congress Control Number:
2002103413

ISBN 0-9717080-4-5
Hardcover version

ISBN 0-9717080-5-3
Softcover version

Printed in the United States of America
by Walsworth Publishing Co., Inc.
Marceline, Missouri

Dust jacket/cover: This four-hour exposure, made in
Johnson County, Missouri, captured the light trails of
stars circling Polaris, the north star. As the earth turns,
stars appear to us to rise and set the same way the
sun does in the daytime, moving from east to west.
Photographic time exposure makes the stars appear
to be streaking by, even though it is Earth that is
turning.

Introduction photos:
i: Aurora Borealis, photographed March
2001, in Johnson County, Kansas.
ii: Comet Hale-Bopp, photographed March
16, 1997, at Powell Botanical Gardens,
Johnson County, Missouri.
iv-v: Milky Way, composite photograph
made in June 1999 in Bolivia.

7/03

CONTENTS

Acknowledgments • Weather tips • Spring sky chart • Winter sky chart • Astronomical viewing tips • North American eclipse paths • The authors • Photo credits

Harbinger of stormy weather: Cumulonimbus cloud crowned by a well-defined anvil shape over the Kansas City area.

INTRODUCTION

The skies between the Rocky Mountains and the Mississippi River bring out nature's best. From the lowest clouds, stratus, to the highest clouds that we can see, cirrus, to the planets and the stars and the entire universe, we can experience just about everything right here in the heartland of the United States.

As a weathercaster in Kansas City for the last 11 years I have watched the sky continually. Each morning, the first thing I do is look outside and up to see what brilliance nature has to offer. Every day is unique. Every day is exciting as we venture into its uncertainties.

Are there signs of a change in the weather? How about a gorgeous sunrise? Are the clouds up there the kind that will create a beautiful horizon — or do they tell of an approaching storm?

And there's much more of interest in the sky, things that don't pertain to weather. Is the moon waxing or waning? Is that bright star on the horizon the planet Venus, or is it a Supernova? Did you see the tremendous Aurora Borealis?

In this book, we'll show you fantastic photographs of what the universe offers the naked eye — and some of what you can see only with optical help. We'll tell you what's going on in those images — for instance, what cloud formations mean. Did you know that you can forecast the weather with some accuracy just by looking at the sky?

You'll see sunrises and clouds and the sun close up, and awesome storms over the plains. You'll see splendid scenes in the night sky — out there in what seems like darkness beyond the earth's atmosphere.

Ever since age 5, I've been interested in the sky. The first small cumulus cloud I remember seeing filled me with excitement. Soon, I realized that those small clouds changed shapes and often began to grow. Now, I know that an approaching cold front — or the day's heat — may deliver enough energy to produce hail, squalls, lightning and maybe even a tornado. All that can occur within hours of the time you first spot that little cumulus cloud.

And in a matter of minutes the thunderstorm can wither as downdrafts take over and the violence fades away. Then the sky clears and just a few clouds are left — to create a beautiful sunset.

As the sky turns dark, the stars appear. Do you know what the Milky Way is? Have you seen it? We'll show you the vast array of the night sky.

If you're an amateur astronomer, a weather enthusiast, or a professional — or if you've ever simply marveled at the stars and the clouds and the moon and the planets — this book will open your eyes. You and your friends and your family will return often to the daily spectacle in the skies above the heartland.

— Gary Lezak

ABOUT THIS BOOK

The spectacular photographs you are about to see were made over the last couple of decades using modern optical equipment. The text you're about to read is current, based on the latest scientific knowledge.

Occasionally accompanying this modern information are the words of people who passed this way long ago — some of them more than a century and a half ago. They were nomads, explorers, pioneers, and thinkers with this in common: They were imaginative, they recorded what they thought and saw, and they spent time here in the heart of North America.

Their knowledge of meteorology and astronomy was primitive compared with ours . Yet the meaning of skies, clouds and stars was far more important in their lives. These long-ago midwesterners traveled dusty trails on foot or horseback, slept beneath covered wagons, lived in makeshift cabins that were poorly sealed against cold, unprotected against heat and leaky in rain or snow. They experienced more or less directly and more or less constantly scorching sun, threatening lightning, brutal winds and bitter cold.

To them the skies above transcended mere description. The skies they witnessed were the stuff of life.

DAWN

"We have glorious risings and settings of the sun....
The rich sunlight, bathing the clouds in gold, spreads
over valley and river."

— James F. Meline, June 17, 1866. From Two Thousand Miles on Horseback:
Santa Fe and Back: A Summer Tour Through Kansas, Nebraska, Colorado
and New Mexico, in the Year 1866.

"Nature has this morning put on her gay green livery.
The Sun rising in Golden Splendor. Cool and pleasant day."

— William Walker in his daily journal of Sept. 2, 1852, written in Indian Territory, in Wyandott nation lands a few miles west of the Town of Kansas.

The dawning of the day may bring low-lying stratus clouds or fog with a deck of higher cirrus clouds across the western sky. An old rhyme goes:

Red sky at morning, sailors take warning.
Red sky at night, sailors delight.

There's truth in it. High- and middle-level clouds can be illuminated by the sun's first rays as much as 30 minutes before sunrise. That's because red light has a long wavelength; red rays from the sun can bend around the Earth's curvature and light clouds before the sun tops the horizon. If the illuminated clouds lie on the western horizon opposite the rising sun, they may portend rain, because most storm systems move from west to east.

A red sky in the evening usually indicates the storm is moving away.

Preceding page: Linn County, Kansas

Linn County, Kansas

Johnson County,
Kansas

"The higher the clouds,
the finer the weather."

"All weather signs fail in
Kansas."

— *Separate bits of weather lore as quoted in*
Folklore from Kansas *by William E. Koch.*

Altostratus is a mid-level cloud thin enough for the sun to shine through. They signify a stable atmosphere and a dry day. A lonely cumulus cloud may form in the afternoon sun.

Strands of cirrus clouds, if they are isolated, signify a wonderful day. Often these clouds, which are 20,000 feet up in the sky or higher, look like the skeleton of a fish.

If all you see are cirrus clouds, it's likely that high pressure is covering the area. That usually means clear, dry weather — weather that can last days or even weeks before the next storm arrives.

As the sun sneaks behind a large cumulus cloud it may produce the proverbial silver lining as it shines through the top of the billowing castle in the sky. Strong upward motion is evident in these clouds, the indicator of a developing Midwestern thunderstorm.

Miami County, Kansas

A rare cirrocumulus cloud about 20,000 feet up.

Turbulence is evident in these cumulonimbus mammatus clouds. Rain is falling from a nearby thunderstorm.

Altostratus. The sun casts a shadow under thin cirrus clouds.

Clouds can occur from the ground all the way up to 70,000 feet. Meteorologists classify clouds in three primary categories and 10 types. An English meteorologist, Luke Howard, in 1803 proposed a system to describe the cloud types with Latin names and we still use it.

Cumulus describes a heap of clouds, stratus a featureless layer, and cirrus a wispy filament. The Latin word nimbus is used as a prefix or suffix with the other terms. It means "rain." Alto describes middle-level clouds. From these words the 10 main cloud types are named.

Stratus is the lowest cloud; its base can be as low as the ground up to about 3,000 feet above the Earth's surface. These gray clouds are usually a smooth, featureless blanket, most often composed of tiny condensed water droplets.

Cirrus are the highest clouds. They're composed of ice crystals, and look like wisps. They exist at heights of 20,000 feet and above.

Cumulus can span the entire lower atmosphere, with a base at 2,000 to 6,000 feet and tops as high as 70,000 feet. They can become cumulonimbus, the largest cloud type, the cloud that is most often a thunderstorm and the only kind that can produce hail.

Here are the 10 types of clouds.

■ Low-lying: stratus, stratocumulus and cumulus.

■ Mid-level: altocumulus and altostratus.

■ High: cirrus, cirrostratus, and cirrocumulus.

■ Low to high: nimbostratus and cumulonimbus. Notice how nimbus occurs in the two types from which moisture can fall.

There are many variations, but if you learn these cloud types you'll begin to understand how the weather works.

Facing page and above: Johnson County, Kansas

THE SUN

Wa kon ta Hum pa to.

The God Of Day

"Grandfather."

> — *Osage name for the sun. From* Osage
> Indian Customs and Myths
> *by Louis F. Burns*

"Noon out on the wide prairie. The sun it seems is exerting himself; not a breath of air is stirring, and everything is scorching with heat."

> — *Susan Shelby Magoffin on the fifth day of her journey from Independence, Missouri, to Santa Fe. From her diary, June 15, 1846.*
> *From* Down the Santa Fe Trail and Into Mexico.

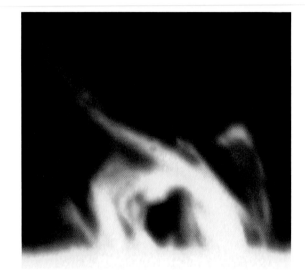

No single object or force dominates our lives like our sun.

For centuries, the sun was our clock from its rising in the morning to its setting at night. We measured our days by observing its shadow. The sun also gave us our seasons, marking the time for farmers to plant and to harvest.

It warms our oceans to make currents and evaporates water to cause rain. It shines rays of energy that not only warm us but also feed nearly every living thing on Earth.

If its light blinked out tomorrow, our planet would instantly become dark and soon cold. But rest assured: the sun won't burn out any time soon. It's been around for five billion years and is expected to last five billion more.

A sun halo, right, is a beautiful example of the prism effect of sunlight through ice. Tiny six-sided ice crystals are shaped with precisely angled sides. When light enters a crystal it leaves at an angle — called refraction. Different colors of light bend at slightly different angles, spreading the light of a sun halo into a circular rainbow. All these crystals bend light at identical angles. Typically, a sun halo is 22 degrees wide.

Only with special protective filters can astronomers — or anyone — safely look directly at the sun. Trying to observe the sun without a filter can cause eye damage or blindness. These images were taken using special astronomical solar filters designed for safe viewing.

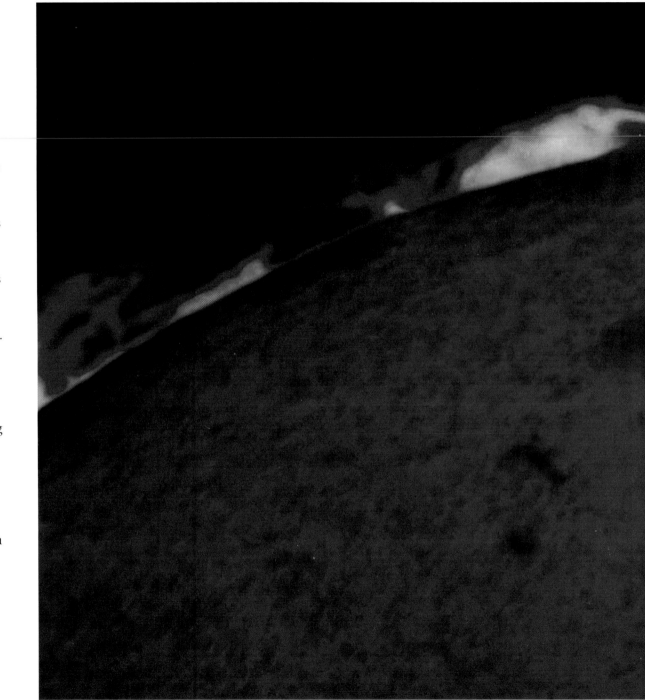

The sun is our nearest star — and a very ordinary star in the context of the entire universe. Luckily, we have a close-up view of the sun, and to us it's a fiery giant. The sun's surface blazes at just above 10,000 degrees Fahrenheit. It is a boiling inferno of hydrogen and helium with sunspots, cooler than the surrounding surface, that are up to 70,000 miles in diameter. Besides light and heat, the sun sends a stream of charged particles called solar winds constantly outward at 280 miles a second. These winds travel through our solar system virtually unnoticed.

Meanwhile, powerful magnetic forces tear openings in its surface, releasing energy in the form of solar flares. Their glowing gases, blasting thousands of miles upward, become a prominence. Most prominences meet the resistance of a magnetic field, which traps them and forces them back toward the sun. If an eruption is large enough and powerful enough to break free, it lofts energy into the solar system and sometimes toward Earth.

"It is said that by some late observations ... there are large spots on the sun's disc. What has come over old Father Sol, that he should now, in his old days, become so silly and vain as to resort to daubing his face with paint!"

— *William Walker in his journal, July 1, 1847.*

Eclipses occur regularly around the world, and they are embedded in folklore. Many cultures regarded a total eclipse as a portent of bad fortune in the struggle between good and evil, light and darkness. A common theory was that the sun was being eaten.

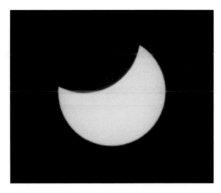

To this day, superstition discourages millions of people from going outside during an eclipse. One Indian wise man warned his followers not to look at the sun during the eclipse or their souls would be changed forever. Modern-day observers who have seen the sun in total eclipse would agree: in a way, his statement is true.

"Right at noon, when people were starting to eat dinner, it began to get dark. It got darker and darker.... All the people were frightened.... 'The sun is dying!' they yelled. 'A snake has come up from under the world and is swallowing the sun!' "

— ``Kiowa George" Poolaw, recalling the story of a 19th-century eclipse for interviewers in the 1930s. From Plains Indian Mythology by Alice Marriott and Carol K. Rachlin.

Only once in about 400 years does a total eclipse of the sun occur at any one spot on Earth. The last total eclipse in our area came in 1806. Some called it Tecumseh's eclipse because its coming was said to have been foretold by the Indian chief.

Since 1806, midwesterners have had to travel hundreds or thousands of miles to be inside the 100-mile-wide path called totality, where the sun's disk is completely blocked. The photograph on this page was taken in Turkey, the one on the facing page in Madagascar.

In 2017 this once-in-a-lifetime event is due to head our way again. That may like a long time away, but compared with 400 years it's right around the corner.

A solar eclipse can last for several hours after the moon's silhouette first touches the sun. Totality can last from a few seconds to as long as seven minutes and 40 seconds.

In the first, partial phase of a solar eclipse, there is little visible change in the sky's brightness. In the few minutes before totality, light and colors and shadows begin to wane. At the last moment, a single, piercing beam of light escapes between mountains on the edge of the moon; the result is the brilliant image of a glistening diamond ring.

Instantly, wispy streamers appear. These beautiful white, wafting shapes are the sun's corona. They are visible to us only then, when the moon's disk entirely blocks the solar disk. Temperatures in the corona are far hotter than on the surface itself — measured in millions of degrees instead of thousands — and scientists are uncertain why.

Within moments, the total eclipse ends. Another diamond-ring image appears briefly and the eclipse becomes partial again.

This glorious event has strongly affected and inspired many who have witnessed it. No still photograph or motion picture can compare with the sensation of experiencing this celestial spectacle live.

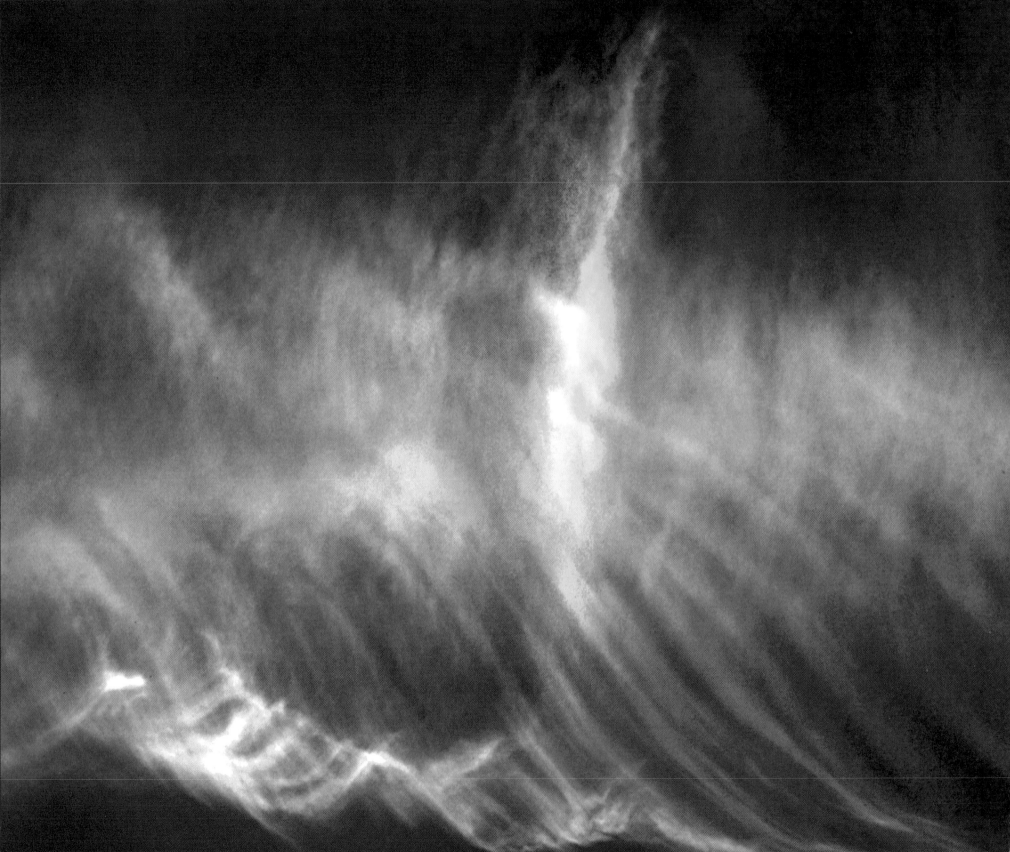

"I have now spent two summers, three autumns, three winters and two springs along the lower Missouri and I must confess that, I do not wish for a better climate. Above all I praise the clear sky."

— Gottfried Duden, German immigrant to Montgomery County, Missouri, in early 1827.

These tiny streaks, like miniature rainbows in the sky, are caused by ice, not rain droplets. Commonly called sundogs, they are sunlight refracted through tiny crystals falling through our upper atmosphere. These crystals are shaped like hexagonal plates, and they tend to flatten out when falling through the air. The light refracted through them is aimed to the side, creating to our eyes a matched set of two rainbow-colored streaks to the left and right of the sun.

STORM

"Such sharp and incessant flashes of lightning, such stunning and continuous thunder I had never known before. The woods were completely obscured by the diagonal sheets of rain that fell with a heavy roar, and rose in spray from the ground."

— *Francis Parkman in Jackson County, Missouri, spring 1846.*
Recounted in The Oregon Trail.

"I doubt if there is any known region out of the tropics than can 'head' the great prairies in 'getting up' thunder-storms, combining so many of the elements of the awful and sublime."

— *Josiah Gregg, telling his experiences on the Santa Fe trail in the 1830s.*

From Commerce of the Prairies.

On a spring or summer day a small, innocent-looking cumulus cloud can grow into an enormous cumulonimbus cloud. Sometimes these clouds have anvil-shaped tops, sometimes not. Stormy weather is on the way.

The first small cloud that forms weighs 1 to 1.5 billion pounds. How does such a heavy object stay afloat in the sky? Dry air — clear sky — weighs more than moist air — water vapor. No more than a slight updraft of rising air will suspend the cloud. Air can rise for several reasons — turbulence from a wind shift, a mountain range, or a pocket of hot air. As the air rises, it cools, condenses and forms cumulus clouds.

When a north wind meets a south wind at the ground, for instance, the air can't go down, so it goes up. With enough moisture, a thunderstorm will begin to form.

At more than a billion pounds, a cumulus cloud is heavy, but a cumulonimbus cloud can weigh more than a thousand times more. Eventually, the updrafts that cause the cumulus clouds to grow into cumulonimbus will be replaced by downdrafts of rain falling in large drops — and perhaps hail. The weight of the cloud in the form of water vapor is transformed into rain that pummels the ground.

Facing page and above, Miami County, Kansas

W hat appears from the ground to be a layer of stratocumulus clouds is often deceiving. The rolling layers obscuring the sky may well be just the bases of cumulonimbus clouds growing above. Each ripple of clouds visible from below indicates a developing tower of cumulus clouds above. Rain, lightning, and thunder may be only minutes away.

Stanton County, Kansas

Neosho County, Kansas

One of nature's most spectacular clouds forms on the underside of a cumulonimbus cloud. It's called a cumulonimbus mammatus, and it's caused by sinking air pockets in the cloud above. Although similar features can be found in other cloud types, it is most often seen under the anvils of intense thunderstorm clouds. These features become prominent when the sun angle is low.

"It was an avalanche sweeping out of heaven. Nature, in her chariot of storm, rode in terrible majesty....

Clay County, Missouri

Riley County, Kansas

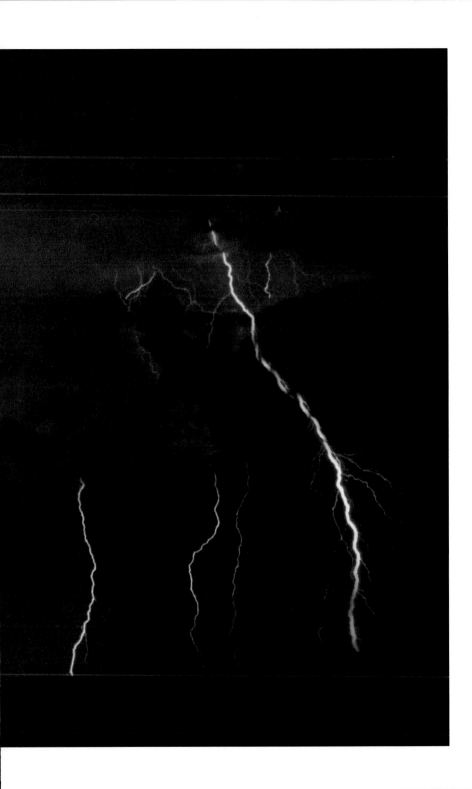

"...Riven trees groaned aghast, and the adjacent mounds were literally plowed with lightnings. Flickering, burning, brightening, the hail-torn air seemed on flame....

Linn County, Kansas

Only one kind of cloud produces lightning — stormy cumulonimbus. First, ice forms in the cloud. If updrafts and downdrafts are strong enough, the cloud's electric charges separate and lightning strikes. Cloud-to-cloud lightning is the most common type, but cloud-to-ground lightning is the most dangerous. Lightning can originate in the cloud, or it can begin on the ground.

Sound travels about a mile in five seconds, much slower than light. If you see lightning and then hear thunder five seconds later, the lightning is about a mile away. Lightning becomes more frequent in the strongest thunderstorms. Only these stronger thunderstorms can produce tornadoes.

"...It was wordlessly awful."

— Max Greene, writing about a storm he saw in Jackson County, Missouri, in the 1850s. From The Kanzas Region: Forest, Prairie, Desert, Mountain, Vale, and River.

In the early 1980s, working on the photo desk of an Oklahoma newspaper, I waited for a storm like this to happen. Each tornado season, a newsroom colleague and I listened avidly to the police radio. When we heard a tornado had been spotted near Copan, Okla., we jumped in the car and headed north, following the reports across the state line into Kansas. By the time we reached Coffeyville, tornado sirens were blaring.

Then we heard the report that 15 head of cattle had vanished. The twister must be close, I thought. We raced past a half-dozen police cars parked on the side of the street, all with lights spinning.

A few miles outside Coffeyville we caught up with the tornado, just in time to see it cross the road a mile or so ahead. We bounced along a side road, parallel with the path of the tornado, until our vehicle dipped into a low-water crossing. When we came up the other side, the air was calm and still. Something strange was going on.

The tornado had disappeared. We stopped and got out. Golf ball-sized hail fell as we looked in every direction for the missing twister.

Then we noticed the rain.

All around us, raindrops were spinning, but they did not fall. We heard a deep, low moan overhead.

"Shouldn't we get in a ditch or something?" my companion implored, his eyes hollow and his face sheet-white.

"Nah; it's headed that way," I said, pointing at the spinning rain as it shifted away. Happily, I was right. We saw the twister re-form and descend again to the ground. It filled instantly with dust and headed toward a farmhouse. The farmhouse looked to be doomed, but the tornado bounced off the ground and hopped over it, as if in a heart-stopping game of leapfrog. I quickly snapped 10 or 15 shots of the tornado. This was one of them.

Then, just as quickly as the tornado appeared, it was gone.

— Vic Winter

Osage County, Oklahoma

Johnson County, Kansas

"And the red elms by the streamlets

Caught the fading evening gleamlets

That in proof,

Gave the token

That the summer storm was broken."

— From ``The Prairie Storm" by Ironquill, pen name of the 19th-century
southeast Kansas poet Eugene Ware.

Preceding pages: Linn County, Kansas

"One evening a great rainbow flashed through the sun-lit rain. It was so big and so lovely! I called out to mother .... Turning and facing the red splendor, she cried out in delight."

— *Memory of Marian Russell on her first trip along the Santa Fe trail in 1852. From* Land of Enchantment: Memoirs of Marian Russell Along the Santa Fe Trail

Linn County, Kansas

A stormy day often ends with a beautiful rainbow. For you to see it, the sun must be behind you and the rain in front of you. Most of the light from the sun passes through the rain, but some of it is reflected back toward you, each color at a different angle through the spectrum. That's why we get so many beautiful colors in a rainbow.

Once the storm has passed, the air usually becomes cooler and more stable. Warm, humid air has been replaced and replenished by the rain-cooled air from above.

"The storm clearing away at about sunset opened a noble prospect....The sun streamed from the breaking clouds."

— *Francis Parkman in Jackson County, Missouri, spring 1846.*

A stormy-looking sky may bring no rain or snow at all. These stratocumulus clouds, for instance, have grown taller, but not quite enough to form into thunderstorms. The nature of these clouds is called stratiform, or spreading out, and it indicates that the atmosphere is becoming more stable. They can, nevertheless, create a threatening landscape at the end of the day.

Linn County, Kansas

What will tomorrow bring? Is it going to rain or snow? Will it be sunny and warmer tomorrow? If you gaze into the sky and can identify what you see, you can develop skills that will help you forecast the weather.

A storm may be 2000 miles away, yet if you look to the western horizon you may see evidence of impending rain 24 to 36 hours before it arrives. Do you see a wispy, high cirrus cloud, and is it moving west to east? Check it again every three hours. If a storm is approaching, that cirrus cloud will spread out and thicken, becoming the more extensive cloud we call cirrostratus.

Then middle-level clouds, altostratus and altocumulus, will begin to form below. For a while, the sun may be dimly visible through them. In just a few hours, the sky may thicken to overcast and the sun will disappear.

Rapid thickening, in less than six hours, can signal the approach of a storm system — meteorologists call it an upper-level disturbance — meaning rain or snow within 24 hours.

And there are other indicators of storms. One is the direction of the wind. Wind blows toward low pressure and away from high pressure. A low-pressure area is usually associated with stormy weather. A high-pressure area usually indicates a sunny sky. A wind from the east or the southeast, therefore, tells you a low-pressure area is to your west. Get ready for precipitation.

Then there's barometric pressure. If the pressure is falling, and the winds are coming from the east, and the clouds are rapidly thickening as described above, it's likely a storm is approaching. If the pressure is rising, and the winds are from the west, expect high pressure to move in, bringing clear skies.

Let's take another example. Say it's a sunny spring day, mid-afternoon under a blue sky. Before you know it, a high overcast has spread in the sky.

These cirrus clouds may form the advance guard of a thunderstorm. They're at the top of a towering cumulonimbus cloud. They take the shape of an anvil, and are carried along by the jet stream. The cumulonimbus clouds carrying thunderstorms may still be hundreds of miles away. When they arrive, the weather should turn exciting — to say the least!

Yet they may not strike your area. Thunderstorms can dissipate even while their high-flying anvil clouds advance across the sky.

Towering cumulus clouds frame the sun — foreshadowing twin thunderstorms

SUNSET

"Evening after evening we watched the prairie sun go
down in its glory, and then watched the white stars
shine in the night above us."

— *Marian Russell, recalling her first trip on the Santa Fe trail in 1852.*

OUR SPACIOUS SKIES

A blue sky turns to gold before our eyes, thanks to the rays of a setting sun. Twice each day, in fact, we may be able to marvel at crayon-colored skies, every color of the rainbow.

Why is the sky blue, when the sun isn't? Children ask the question; do you know the answer? After all, we know that the sun sends a full spectrum of color in every ray.

The reason is that waves of different-colored light in the spectrum are different lengths. Red, orange and yellow light have longer wavelengths and pass right through. Blue and violet wavelengths are short and are absorbed by gases, then radiated in all directions. Scattered as the blue and violet light has been, we look up to see a sky filled with that color.

Unlike sunlight at other times, rays of a setting sun must pass through a lot of thick atmosphere. Longer wavelengths can more easily pass through it and bend around the curve of the Earth. Red, the longest, is the last color visible at sunset because it can bend after other colors can't any longer. It's as if these colors have patiently waited the whole day for blue to fade. Now, they blaze even brighter in this, their brief turn to rule the sky.

Facing page and above: Linn County, Kansas

Colorado

Linn County, Kansas

"Each sunset is declared more magnificent than the last."

— James F. Meline in Two Thousand Miles on Horseback

The sky is dimming and colors fade. The evening settles into tranquility. As if it's fading quietly into sleep, the day slips into twilight. Shadows rise and grow tall around us until they are not shadows at all, but darkness. The hour of dusk is patient, softly waiting for the last scattered rays of light to drain from the sky. New actors begin to appear on the heavenly stage. First, a shining planet glimmers on the horizon. Then, a star appears.

Star light, star bright
First star I see tonight.
I wish I may, I wish I might
Have this wish I wish tonight.

As if by a silent wish, the sky begins to open wide, glittering with treasure of boundless stars and galaxies. We can count them for eternity and count them again; each time discovering more new worlds than ever before.

Linn County, Kansas

NIGHT

"Your admiration deepens nightly at
the serenity of the firmament, from
whose massive blue the magnificent
stars come bursting out like red-hot
diamonds."

— *From* The Kanzas Region *by Max Green, 1856.*

"In the night Ursa Major (the Great Bear) is not only useful to find the north star, but its position, when the pointers will be vertical in the heavens, may be estimated with sufficient accuracy to determine the north even when the north star cannot be seen."

— *From* The Prairie Traveler *by Randolph Barnes Marcy, Captain, U.S.A., 1859.*

Everyone needs to know how to find the North Star, Polaris. It's not by any means the brightest star in our sky. But it is unique in the heavens. No matter what time of night, what day, what month or what year, it appears to us to be standing still. Here's why:

Imagine that Earth has an invisible rod on which it spins, the same way a globe does. One end of the rod goes through the North Pole, the other through the South Pole. In the northern hemisphere, our imaginary rod points right at Polaris. That's why Polaris marks true north. For thousands of years, people have used it to find their way.

But how do we find Polaris? First, let's find the constellation Ursa Major, commonly known as the Big Dipper. It looks like a giant ladle, or dipper in the sky. The Big Dipper is easy to find on the right side of this photograph, standing on the end of its handle. Depending on the time and the season, it may also appear upside-down or right-side up.

Next, find the two stars at the Big Dipper's front edge. A line between them points to Polaris. It's as if the North Star had been spilled from the Big Dipper.

Polaris lies at the end of the handle in Ursa Minor, the Little Dipper, but this constellation is not always easy to find in the sky, particularly over bright cities. The Big Dipper is more visible and a more certain means of finding your way.

As Earth rotates, stars appear to move across the night sky from east to west. The naked eye can only tell that constellations have shifted over time. Photographic film, however, documents the movement and the trails of light left by stars. To make the photograph of star trails, left, the shutter was left open for two hours.

"Your admiration deepens nightly at the serenity of the firmament, from whose massive blue the magnificent stars come bursting out like red-hot diamonds."

— *From* The Kanzas Region *by Max Green, 1856.*

Cherry County, Nebraska

Many adults remember a time in their childhood when they lay in the grass and gazed up at the night sky. Back then, the stars twinkled like diamonds. Today, our city sky is only a hazy reminder of those memories. Unfortunately, the skies in our neighborhoods today are generally flooded by outdoor lighting. Stray light from street lights, porch lights or illuminated billboards bounces endlessly among drops of humidity in the night air. Only major constellations and clusters of stars like the Pleiades, above, are left to discern.

The photograph on the facing page shows how a single light can fog a few hundred yards of air. The glow in the sky above our cities is far more extensive. That's why astronomers today must head to the countryside. Most of nighttime photos in this book were taken from places outside the city and far from its lights. These patches of dark sky needed to observe and photograph the stars are, unhappily, shrinking every year.

Children who grow up in the city today probably will never see the Milky Way from their backyards the way adults remember. We hope you'll escape the glare of city lights with your children and really see the stars. Meanwhile, remember to turn off outdoor lights you're not using. Then you can look up and share the night sky with your friends and family.

Facing page: Johnson County, Missouri

Late on a summer evening, a faint trail of irregular light flows gently across our darkened sky. If you're away from bright city lights, the name Milky Way will take on an impressive meaning. This bumpy spine of white stellar patches — described by some as steam from the teapot in the constellation Sagittarius — is endlessly fascinating. You're seeing billions of other stars, and also the dust, gas and nebulae that comprise the Milky Way galaxy, a vast pinwheel.

Our solar system is a passenger in one arm of that pinwheel, which is spinning about 486,000 miles an hour around the galaxy's core. At midsummer, with the Milky Way stretched horizon to horizon, we are peering inward through the plane of our own galaxy to its arms and core. An estimated 586,971,360,000,000 miles across, our solar system makes a full revolution in about 226,000,000 years.

This image, a composite of four time-exposure photographs, captures the colors of the Milky Way. To the unaided eye, the galaxy will appear far less colorful.

Peering deeper into the night with optical assistance, what appeared to the naked eye as faint and fuzzy blurs now evolve into shapes. A good pair of binoculars reveals different colors among the stars, and shows moons orbiting Jupiter. The night sky abounds in bright and colorful treasures — for those who reach to explore it.

An amateur astronomer can expect to see globular clusters with uncountable stars bunched together. Spiral galaxies become real when we see their whirlpool shapes through the eyepiece of a telescope. Dust and gas form nebulas with faint, glowing colors, right. Just as we see animal shapes in clouds, or a dog in the stick figure of a constellation, nebulas often take recognizable shapes, and are named after them. It doesn't take much imagination to see how the North American, Horsehead and Witchhead nebulas got their names.

A telescope surprises viewers with a show of Saturn's rings, sometimes so crisp they seem painted in the sky. Fantastic images become vivid reality when we can gaze deep inside the constellation Orion to find the blazing wings of the Great Orion Nebula, left.

WANDERERS

"On the evening of Dec. 21st, 1876, a very large and remarkable meteor … passed over the central belt of the United States …. Observers at Pleasant Hill, Missouri, say it emitted sparks just before it disappeared below the horizon and produced a light greater than moonlight."

— Western Review of Science and Industry, *edited by Theodore S. Case*
and published in Kansas City, February, 1877.

C O M E T S

Comets are icy visitors from millions of miles away. They come from the frozen Kuiper Belt, a band of disorganized material extending beyond Neptune, and the Oort Cloud, a halo of material beyond the solar system. Comets are like dirty snowballs. They're composed of frozen dust and gas. Once the sun's gravity pulls a comet close enough, the ice begins to melt, forming a halo around the core of the comet. More melting releases tails, a gas tail and a dust tail. Gas tails can extend thousands of miles and dust tails millions of miles behind the comet. Some comets visit our skies once and are gone. For others we can calculate their returns for hundreds, even thousands, of years.

A comet's path can change if it comes too near objects in our solar system. The gravity of a large planet can pull a comet, altering its course forever. Astronomers scan the sky every day and night, looking for comets and calculating their paths. With a good telescope, you can ordinarily see several comets at any time.

Many comets are discovered by amateur astronomers. Once a comet is discovered and confirmed, it receives the name of the astronomer who found it first. The next great comet discovery may be only a few nights away!

The world chanced to see several incredible comets in the 1990s. They were powerful and exciting discoveries — particularly after the disappointing display by the renowned Halley's Comet in 1986.

One astounding comet was Hale-Bopp, which astronomers saw coming from far out in space. When it swooped out from behind the sun, Hale-Bopp, left and right, boasted a fantastic pair of ion and dust tails. Visible to the naked eye, the comet dominated science news for months. With a telescope, the beautiful plasma tail and dust trail made a giant "V" shape.

Best captured on film, comet Hale-Bopp's tails were vivid blue and reddish-yellow. Millions of people flocked to observatories to see the comet in spring 1997; many were disappointed when the comet eventually disappeared from view.

Jackson County, Missouri

Facing page: Washington County, Oklahoma

Comet Hyakutake passed remarkably close to earth in 1996. Its route was nearly perpendicular to the plane of our solar system and supplied extraordinary views of its tail. After circling the sun and being warmed by it, Hyakutake's tail grew to more than 68,000,000 miles in length by astronomers' estimates. In only a few months, the comet blazed back out of the solar system. The happy encounter left many astronomers believing they had witnessed a once-in-a-lifetime event.

Facing page and above: Johnson County, Missouri

"Between 3 and 4 o'clock on Wednesday morning, November 13, 1833, there occurred in Montgomery County and throughout the whole country a meteoric phenomenon, the splendor of which never passed from those who witnessed it .... An inconceivable number of meteors or falling stars shot across and downward from the heavens, as though the whole framework of the blue and cloudless arch had been shaken."

— *History of St. Charles, Montgomery and Warren Counties, Missouri*

Did you know that you've seen meteors fall? Informally they're called shooting stars, yet they're not stars at all. Shooting stars are specks of space debris that happen into our atmosphere and blaze a fiery trail before burning away. Most meteors are no larger than a grain of sand or a pea-sized stone, racing along as fast as 100,000 kilometers a second. At that speed, even rock is burned away in the intense heat of friction created by the plunge into earth's atmosphere.

We see meteor showers yearly because comets leave debris along their paths for millions of miles. When Earth passes through a comet's path, we are treated to a cosmic lightshow.

For instance, every year our planet crosses the path of comet Temple-Tuttle, a zone rich in meteors. (The comet itself visits only every 33 years.) When Earth and the comet's path intersect, meteor showers occur. All meteors in the shower appear to move outward from a single spot, a magic point called the radiant. Meteor showers are named for the constellation from which they appear to radiate to us on Earth. When this shower occurs — around Nov. 17 to 20 — you can trace the path of most meteors back to the constellation Leo. The shower is called the Leonid.

When Earth crosses the path of comet Swift-Tuttle each August, meteors appear to radiate from the constellation Perseus. That meteor shower is called the Perseid.

On Earth, a few specks of rock seem insignificant. In space, they create an unforgettable spectacle.

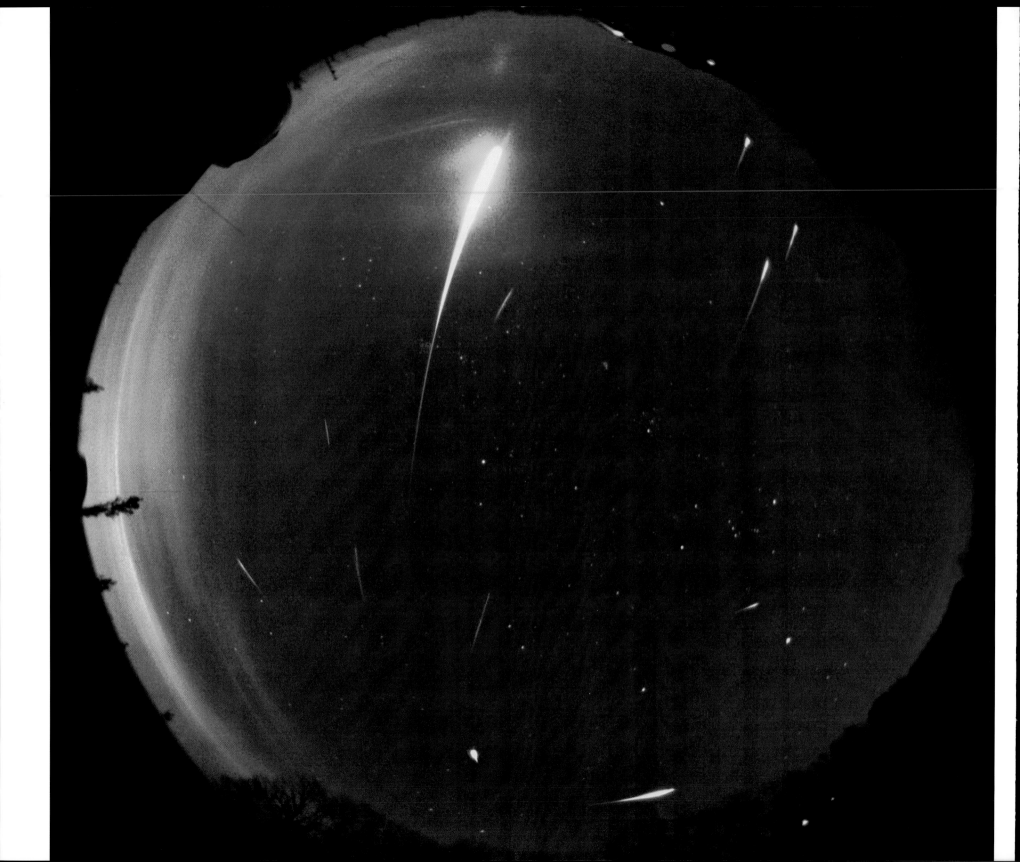

Sometimes a larger chunk of rock hits our atmosphere. Even a stone the size of a golf ball will create a dazzling streak across the night sky. These bigger meteors, called bolides, can be as bright as a full moon. So much material is burned during their descent that they may change colors, break apart and leave a train of ionized gas in their wake. Some trains are visible for a few minutes, some as long as an hour. Bolides are uncommon, but the chance of seeing one is better in a meteor shower.

Even more rare is the chance that the meteor will survive this fiery torture and reach the ground. If it does, it will have been burned to a fraction of its original size and slowed to a fraction of its original speed. Cooling as it slows, the meteor usually falls to the ground unnoticed. Once it strikes the Earth's surface, a meteor is called a meteorite. Meteorites discovered on Earth usually are pieces of other planetary matter. Through such finds, we can investigate and probe other worlds without leaving our own.

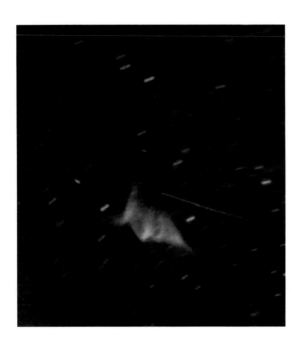

"I was not born then, but my mother was a young woman growing up, and she saw the stars fall out of the sky, and never forgot it.

"One evening a man went out of his wife's tipi. All at once he let out a great shout, 'The stars are falling! The whole sky is falling!'"

— *"Kiowa George" Poolaw retelling stories passed down to him.*

Facing page and above: Johnson County, Missouri

Perhaps an object you saw in the sky last night blinked and moved. Perhaps it was an airplane, but if its light was dim and it looked like a star, the moving object probably was an artificial satellite. These orbiting spacecraft come in many forms and grow in number every year. Most satellites are launched for commercial purposes. Others are government-backed, carrying the valuable payload of our hopes and ambitions to explore the cosmos. Satellites reflect sunlight off their shiny metal surfaces and solar panels back to Earth. We see them as tiny dots moving rapidly across the night sky. The Hubble Space Telescope satellite can be seen from Earth. The Space Shuttle is also a very large, noticeable object. As the International Space Station has grown, we have watched it surpass Venus and become the second brightest object in the nighttime sky.

As if the sky weren't crowded enough, one company beginning in the 1990s has launched 67 communications satellites. They are stationed in a ring around Earth to create a global communications relay system. Each satellite sports a flashy, reflective set of solar panels prone to catch sunlight on every orbit. That reflected flash is now called an Iridium flare, after the name given to the satellites by the company that launched them. Today, we can map their paths and predict exactly when and where we'll see these brilliant surges of light.

The aurora borealis streaked brazenly across the sky in far northern reaches of Earth for centuries, while science struggled to understand it. Now, we look to the sun as the cause. Magnetic storms there release enormous surges of energy into our solar system. With optical help, we can see these eruptions on the edge of the sun, blasting off in ruby-red prominences 10 times the size of Earth. There is enough energy in one eruption to power everything on Earth for more than a century. Often, this energy travels toward Earth. When it arrives, most of the energy is deflected by the natural electromagnetic field surrounding the planet. The North and South poles suffer the brunt of the storm. Gases in our atmosphere are charged by this energy arriving at the poles, glowing like neon in a tube. Different gasses glow and twinkle in streaks of different colors of the rainbow. From below, auroras can snake like icicles on a spiral stairway. From afar, the sky shimmers in muted shades like a curtain fluttering in the night.

The image at upper right, the surface of the sun, was taken March 29, 2001, when an active region of multiple solar flares, named AR region 9393, developed sunspots more than 13 times the size of Earth. Energy released in that eruption reached Earth three days later, on April 1, 2001, spawning auroras that were seen as far south as Texas. These were photographed from Johnson County, Kansas.

E very 11 years magnetic storms on the sun reach their peak. During these solar maximums strong flares, sunspots and enormous coronal ejections translate into strong and widespread auroras on Earth. As our protective geomagnetosphere is pummeled by this energy, it weakens and shrinks, and auroras are seen farther from the poles. This 1991 aurora was photographed in autumn.

Miami County, Kansas

"Of clear evenings, the round moon will float up its path of mellow splendor until the onlooker is drunk to the spirit's core with the red glory that floods half the sky."

— The Kanzas Region: Forest, Prairie, Desert, Mountain, Vale, and River *by Max Greene, 1856.*

Its sliver can be seen in the daytime sky. Its bright orb lights the night. As children, we watched it follow us on our way to grandmother's house. Our moon is a busy heavenly body. It's our closest and perhaps most misunderstood celestial object.

Is the moon larger some times than others? It seems so when seen at the horizon, but that's because trees, hills and other objects are next to it for comparison. High in the sky, there's no earthbound object with which it can be compared.

Through the centuries, various effects have been ascribed to the moon. Some are legendary — the moon does not turn men into werewolves — and some are real — its gravity does tug on Earth's oceans and seas, creating tides.

We know that the moon orbits Earth in an oval, so its apparent size fluctuates slightly — by about 14 percent. We know that the moon revolves on its own axis exactly one time in its orbit around the Earth. That means we see only one side of it. The other side is called the Dark Side, not because it is always dark, but because it escapes our view. We must travel into space to see the other side of Earth's closest neighbor.

The appearance of a man in the moon is caused by the arrangement of the moon's many seas and craters. Those result from the beating that meteors have given the moon through the eons. With no atmosphere for protection, meteors strike the moon at speeds we shudder to comprehend. Yet scarred and battered as it may be, the moon's surface creates beautiful displays of contrast and light for us on Earth.

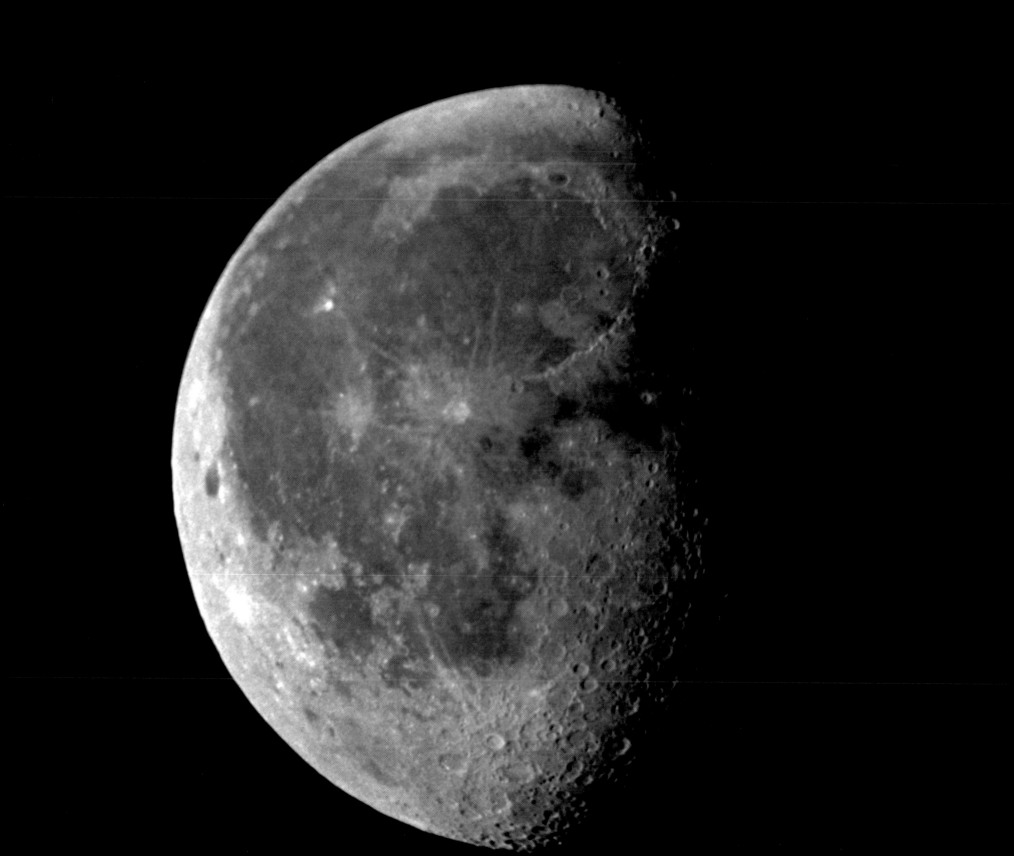

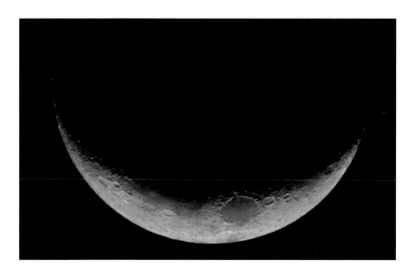

Sometimes the moon is only a sliver creeping toward the setting sun. Other times its full, brilliant disk lights the night like a street lamp. How do these phases of the moon happen? Some people think Earth's shadow is involved, but it's not.

When the moon is on the opposite side of Earth from the sun, all the light reflected off the moon bounces back to the darkened side of Earth. Then we see what we call a full moon. Other nights, when the moon is at Earth's side, we see only part of the moon's sunlit surface. The rest is in darkness.

When the moon is "new," we can't see it because it is positioned between Earth and the sun. Each night, the moon travels about 12 degrees east through the sky. As it does, we begin to see part of the sunlit portion. When the sliver of reflected light begins to grow, we call it the waxing crescent moon.

In a week, half of the moon's face is lit and half is in shadow. This moon is in its first quarter. In another week, the moon is directly opposite the sun from Earth. It rises about the same time the sun sets, and reflecting a full disk of light — a full moon — in its second quarter. Then the moon begins to wane. A gibbous, or humped moon, is more than half full. The last week of the cycle is called a waning crescent moon, slipping back between us and the sun to begin all over again.

This cycle occurs every 29.5 days, the time it takes the moon to orbit Earth.

Earth's shadow usually misses the moon, because the orbits of the two bodies are not parallel. Every once in a while, however, the two align precisely and Earth's shadow covers the moon. This is a lunar eclipse.

In an eclipse, a palette of sunset-colored shades sweeps across the disk of the moon until the moon is covered. Even fully eclipsed, the moon doesn't disappear. Rather, it darkens and changes color. Although the sun's rays are blocked by Earth from striking the moon directly, they bend and refract through Earth's atmosphere and light the moon nevertheless. Also, they're slightly altered by dust and debris in Earth's moist air. So instead of its customary bright self, the moon in eclipse is coated in haunting reds and oranges.

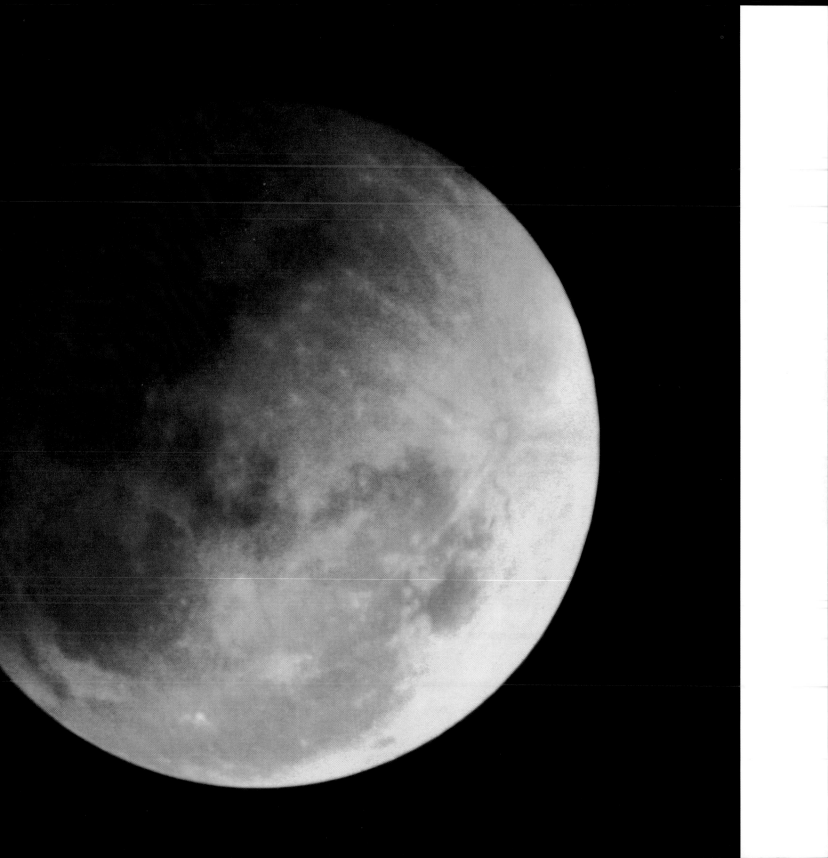

"When there is a ring around the moon, the number of days until a storm will be the same as the number of stars in the ring."

— Folklore from Kansas *by William E. Koch.*

L ike a sun halo, a moon halo is light refracted through crystals in the atmosphere. According to weather folklore, the telltale circle in the sky — a ring around the moon — portends bad weather. That contains some truth.

Those ice crystals signify thin, high-altitude cirrus clouds, which precede a warm front by one or two days. Such fronts often accompany low-pressure systems, which typically cause rain, snow or storms. Indeed, three days after the moon halo on the facing page was photographed, the Kansas City area suffered one of the harshest ice storms in its recorded history.

Folklore has stretched this to say that the number of stars visible inside the halo marks the number of days until the arrival of bad weather. That is, well, only folklore.

Not as large as a moon ring, a moon corona, above, is caused by clouds. It's a colorful display that appears close to the moon, like a daytime rainbow but not as bright because its source is only moonlight. We see moon coronas when the high humidity or when there are light clouds across the moon. A moon corona and a moon ring can occur at the same time — with the correct mix of clouds and crystals.

Johnson County, Kansas

Riley County, Kansas

Each fall, around the equinox in late September, we see a glorious golden full moon rise early in the evening. It's as if the moon is telling us that autumn has arrived and with it harvest time. Indeed, at one time it did. Centuries ago farmers in England noticed that, about that same time each year, they could expect a full moon to rise in the east just as the sun set in the west. The event coincided roughly with their annual harvest, so the harvest moon became a symbol of the season.

You've heard the term, "Once in a blue moon," but do you know what it means — or how often a blue moon happens? The lunar cycle is about every four weeks, and a full moon at each of those intervals. Every month has at least one full moon. If any month has a second full moon, the second is called a blue moon. Unlike the image on the facing page, the phenomenon isn't necessarily blue — just uncommon.

Johnson County, Kansas

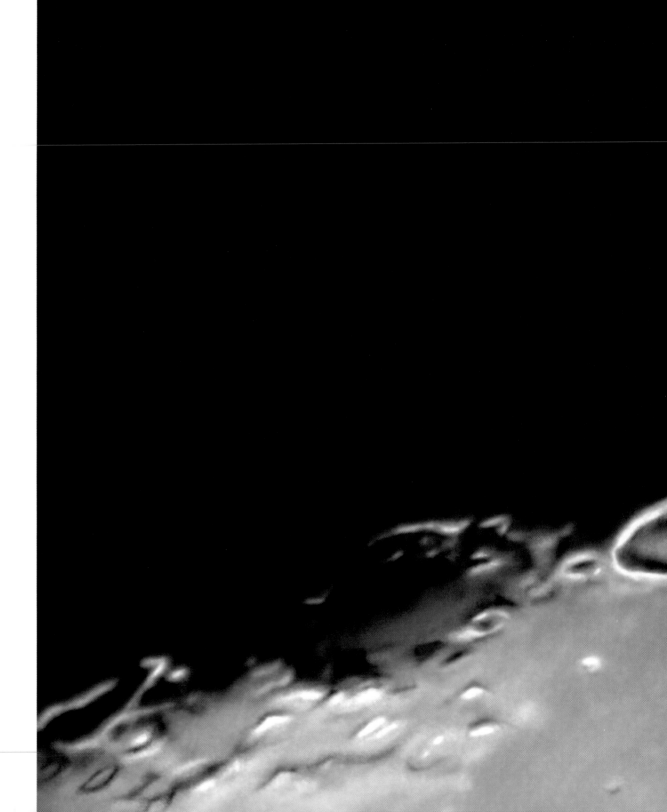

Thousands of years after people began studying the moon, we still don't know precisely what shape it is. We know that it has craters and valleys, but the edges are somewhat fuzzy. Astronomers are sorting this out.

It happens that, as the moon passes bright stars or planets, fine details of its outer shape are revealed. Sometimes the moon covers — or "occults" — a star or other point of light. Other times the two skim each other, the mountains and valleys of the moon alternately hiding and revealing the other object, called "blinking." We can time and map these occultations, which occur year after year, and build a more and more accurate model of the moon's edge.

When the other object is a planet, its meeting with the moon is called a conjunction. Sometimes when the moon occults a planet undiscovered detail is revealed about the planet as well. In 2001, for instance, occultations of Saturn allowed us a rare chance to see its faintest outer rings.

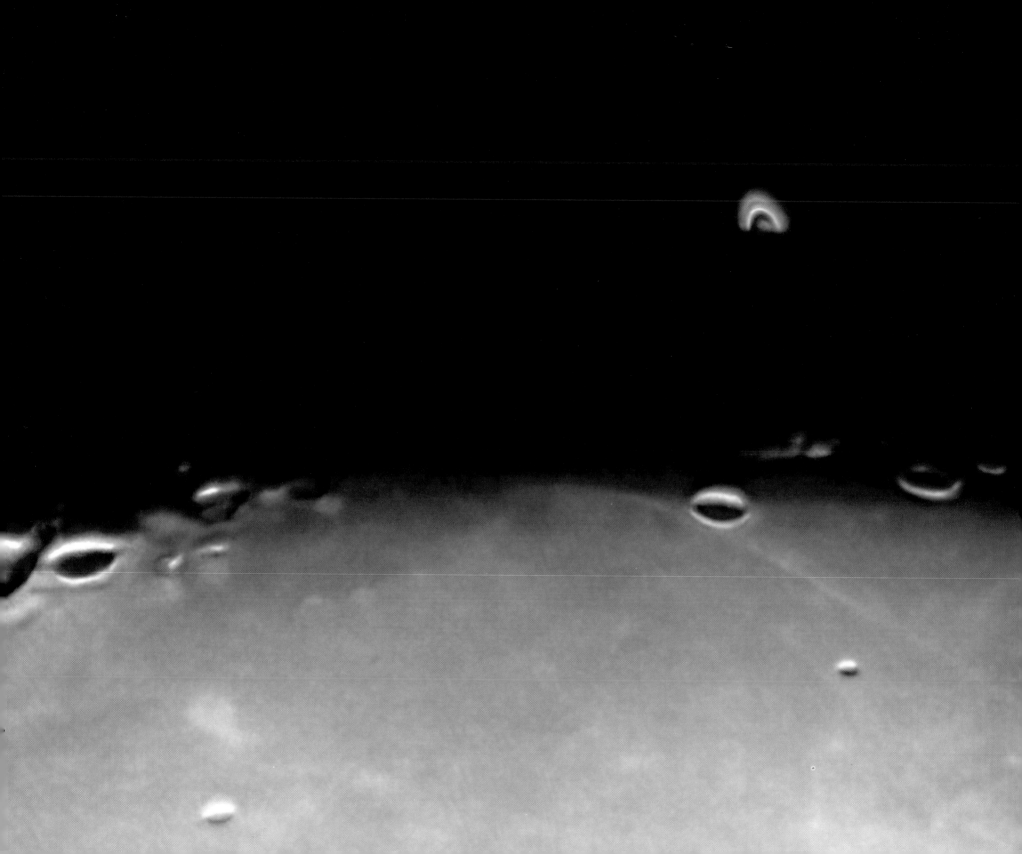

Me Ka he Hun pa to. The morning star.

Meka ke Hun to. The evening star.

— Osage names for Venus, morning and evening.

As long as mankind has looked in wonder at the shapes in the night sky, human beings have sought to understand our place within the heavens. Early Greek philosophers and astronomers began mapping the night sky more than 20 centuries ago. They had no rockets or spacecraft to explore the universe, not even the luxury of a telescope. They were at pains to try to explain a handful of mysterious bright objects in the night sky, objects that didn't move the same way as most stars. The Greeks called these objects wanderers, and from their word for it we get ``planets.''

Planets would become the center of controversy for centuries to come. For many years the prevailing theory held that Earth was the center of the solar system. However, under that theory scholars couldn't explain the orbits of planets.

A revolutionary idea was proposed by an astronomer named Copernicus, and it shook not only science but also western religion to its core. He suggested that Earth — and therefore mankind — was not at the center of the solar system. Instead, Copernicus said, Earth was one of several planets orbiting the sun. Despite objections by the church, time and science proved the theory correct, leaving us to seek a different understanding of our place in the universe.

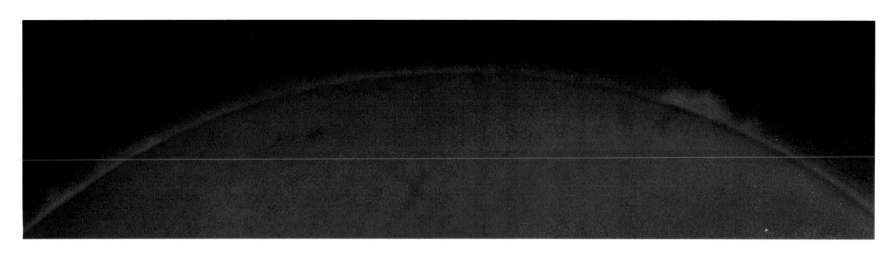

Mercury, the closest planet to the sun, photographed in multiple exposures crossing the solar surface. Mercury and Venus are the only two planets whose orbits lie between Earth and the sun.

Early astronomers measured cosmic distances without computers or telescopes. They mapped the sky carefully and calculated distances by hand. A great deal of effort resulted in a wide understanding of our cosmos.

One nagging difficulty was establishing the precise distance from Earth to the sun. At one time, astronomers hoped the task could be done by triangulation. That required a large object — such as the planet Venus — to move between Earth and the sun. By timing, at different spots on Earth, the intersection of the sun and the object astronomers theoretically could make the necessary calculations. Unfortunately, such an event proved rare. Venus transits the sun about twice every 100 years, and two occur only 12 years apart. In addition, expeditions to remote locations to observe transits were fraught with peril from clouds or even pirates. Ultimately, the experiment proved imprecise. The thick atmosphere of Venus caused light to refract an inconsistent edge of a boiling sun.

This technique has been abandoned and astronomers have found better ways to measure our solar system.

Facing page: Mars, the bright object at lower left, near the Lagoon and Trifid nebulas.

Engrossed by the planet Mars, American astronomer Percival Lowell established the Lowell Observatory in Arizona in the late 19th century. Using its large telescope, he charted what he believed were canals crisscrossing the planet. That required an active imagination, as the photograph of Mars below shows. Based on the supposed existence of canals, Lowell concluded that the planet had at some time contained life — in fact, an advanced civilization of intelligent beings. This poem by Lowell expressed his dream:

One voyage there is I fain would take
While yet a man in mortal make;
Voyage beyond the compassed bound
Of our own Earth's returning round:
Voyage whose shining goal by day
From stupid stare lies hid away
Amid the sun-dimmed depths of space
But when staid night reclaims her sphere
And the beshadowed atmosphere
Its shutters to sight once more unbars,
Letting the universe appear
With all its wonder-world of stars,
My far-off goal draws strangely near,
Luring imagination on,
Beckoning body to be gone —
To ruddy-earthed, blue-oceaned Mars.

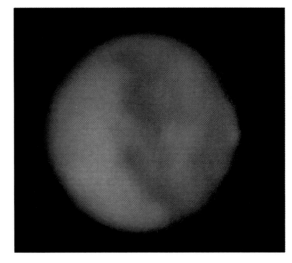

Mars

Facing page: The moon and Venus.

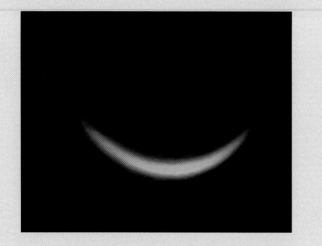

"With a nimbus like a saint
Rose the white moon in the east
And the grass all rose together
As the guests do at a feast....

Just as dawn begins to glow, you may notice a point of light on the eastern horizon. It's bright and close to the ground, and you may take it to be an airplane. Look closer. If it doesn't move, you may have seen a planet — Venus. Venus has been called the morning star and the evening star because it can appear at either time.

After the moon, Venus is the brightest natural celestial object we see at night. That's because it's the next closest object. If you look at Venus through a good pair of binoculars or a telescope, it assumes a crescent shape. When low in the sky, its light refracts in our own atmosphere like a prism causing a striking rainbow of color when examined with a telescope.

"...And the prairie lark kept singing

All the night, and the stirring

And the whizzing and the whirring

Still increased;

Till all sorrow

Yielded to the brilliant morrow."

— *Ironquill*

Dawn's arrival often finds us groggy and weary-eyed. Nevertheless, perhaps we caught a glimpse of zodiacal light, which comes before even the first glimmer of dawn. Zodiacal light, merely a hint of a glow on the eastern horizon, is only a reflection of sunlight on the dust of our solar system. Then the sun's soft glow begins to climb slowly in the eastern sky. As if to gently end the dramatic nighttime show, the sun's light creeps overhead, extinguishing the stars. For a while, twilight lingers. In this quiet hour, we can reflect upon a beautiful night just ended, or the day about to begin.

A C K N O W L E D G M E N T S

These pictures are for you, the curious reader. We took them to share the sky we see with others everywhere. To us, the sky is more than blue-white dots on a black background. We see colorful sundogs, brilliant galaxies and the unexplored hopes and dreams of young astronomers, astronauts and scientists of the future.

These pictures are also for you, our friends — the amateur astronomers and the members of the Astronomical Society of Kansas City. We hope they help recall the moments we have shared, standing together in the dark all these years. Your companionship made even the coldest nights bearable. You were always there to lend a hand moving telescopes, share eyepieces and to inspire us to reach farther through the telescope, year in and year out.

And these pictures are for you, our warm hosts and also the thousands of people we have been privileged to meet in our journeys around the world. We travel thousands of miles from our home to yours to stand beside one another, looking up in awe and wonder at the sky that belongs to us all.

Last but not least, these pictures are for our families. We carry the inspiration of our parents and grandparents in moments that seemed tiny when they passed, but are monumental in retrospect. We only hope our time together can inspire even more interesting dreams onward in our children.

May Starlight Always Fall On Your Path.

In loving memory of Ken Willcox and Charles "Chuck" Douglas.

— Vic Winter
Jen Winter

Thanks to my family and friends who supported me through decades of my weather enthusiasm. And thanks to Vic and Jen Winter for their wonderful work.

— Gary Lezak

Interested in learning more about the weather? You can become a good amateur weather observer by learning a few basics and by purchasing some inexpensive, easy-to-use weather instruments.

Start by going over the cloud types we discussed on Page 13. Learn them and you'll know how to read the fundamental clues of what weather is on the way. From there, you can:

■ Buy an inexpensive rain gauge; you'll find one at most hardware and big variety stores. They're quite accurate.

■ Purchase a barometer and an outdoor thermometer, which can be found in stores and also on the World Wide Web by searching for "weather instruments." The barometer tells you whether the atmospheric pressure is rising or falling. Falling pressure means lower pressure is moving toward you, and low pressure most often is associated with stormy weather. The thermometer will let you track the temperatures and some kinds will let you record the high and low temperatures for the day.

■ Start a weather log. Write down the high and low temperature and the amount of rain or snow each day. Also jot down a few words explaining how you experienced that day's weather.

■ Become a weather observer for your favorite local weather television forecaster.

■ Try making your own forecast. Don't forget rule No. 1 of weather forecasting: Always look outside. You never know what's going to happen, and the weather can change quickly.

There are many web sites on the internet that provide weather forecasts. From them you can gather a trove of weather data — satellite pictures, radar, and temperatures around the region and the nation.

— *Gary Lezak*

Washington County, Oklahoma

Here are two simple star charts, one for summer and one for winter. They show major constellations that are visible in the evening, and are illustrated with the brighter stars. Most of these can be easily seen, even in the city. Larger dots represent brighter stars. The constellations, the work of long-ago imaginations, are connected by lines. More detailed, monthly charts are widely available in popular astronomy magazines and on the internet.

From our vantage point on Earth, the sky appears to move from east to west as the night wears on. Try taking the chart outside right after dark and find the constellations, then return a few hours later to see how things have moved. As seasons change, different constellations appear in our sky.

Pick one of the brightest stars and find it in the sky. Use this as a start to find other stars and constellations. Like the moon, constellations

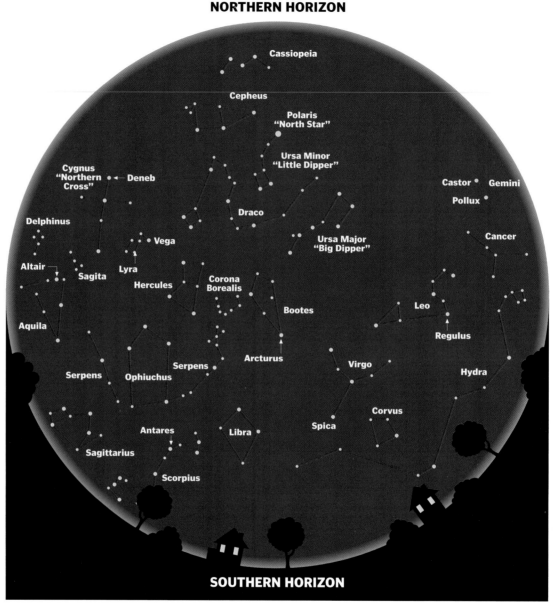

NIGHT SKY IN JUNE

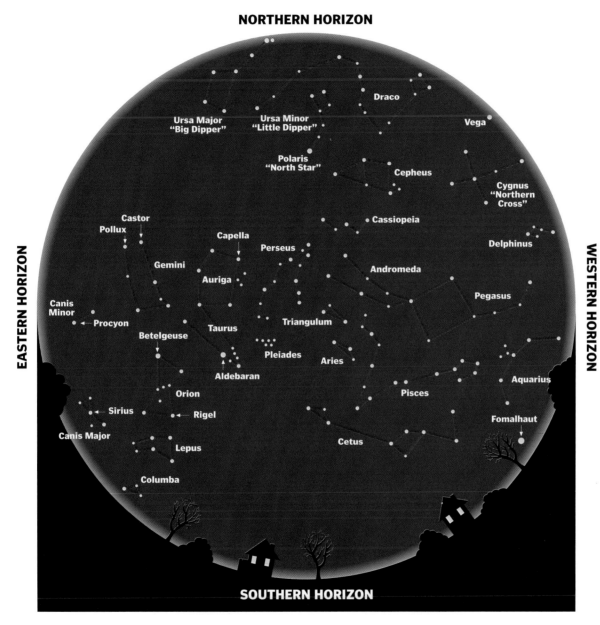

NORTHERN HORIZON

Draco

Ursa Major
"Big Dipper"

Ursa Minor
"Little Dipper"

Vega

Polaris
"North Star"

Cepheus

Cygnus
"Northern
Cross"

Castor

Pollux

Cassiopeia

Delphinus

EASTERN HORIZON

Capella

Perseus

Gemini

Andromeda

Auriga

Pegasus

Canis
Minor

Triangulum

WESTERN HORIZON

Procyon

Taurus

Betelgeuse

Pleiades

Aries

Canis Major

Orion

Aquarius

Sirius

Rigel

Aldebaran

Pisces

Fomalhaut

Lepus

Cetus

Columba

SOUTHERN HORIZON

NIGHT SKY IN DECEMBER

may appear to be much larger when they are near the horizon. They may rise sideways and not straighten out until they are due south. Then they may tilt sideways again when they set.

Some people find that learning constellations is easier in the city because only the brightest stars are visible above bright lights. In the dark of the countryside, a constellation with only 30 stars can become difficult to find in a sky where thousands of stars appear. Until you become more familiar with the night sky, the simple stick figures can melt into a sea of confusion.

Astronomy stores sell more detailed charts. They show the exact location of tens of thousands of objects over many pages. You can also buy computer programs that help you find objects or make your own charts of the sky.

■ Get to know the sky with star charts and a planisphere, which is a map of the night sky with an aid to indicate which part is visible at various times and seasons.

■ Go as far from city lights as possible. The dome of light pollution can extend far beyond your neighborhood.

■ Use a red light! Cover a flashlight with red cellophane or red nail polish. Cover or turn off interior car dome lights. White light will ruin your dark-adapted vision and make it harder to see faint objects. One glimpse of white light can take 20 minutes to recover from.

■ Even moderate-power binoculars reveal hundreds of celestial objects.

■ When purchasing a telescope, buy the best equipment you can afford. You needn't buy the most expensive right away, but remember: In telescopes, quality matters.

■ Take snacks; observing is hard work!

■ Small folding tables are handy for placing observation equipment.

■ If you are observing in a field, take along a small tarpaulin to place under you and your equipment. Not only does it make dropped items easy to find, but also it's good protection from bugs and dew.

■ Find a local astronomy society or club. Members typically are eager to help you learn to explore the sky. Clubs hold regular meetings where you can meet other stargazers and learn about astronomy as a pastime.

■ Visit a public star party. Club newsletters and the internet are filled with opportunities to look at the sky in the company of experienced amateurs. Many clubs offer public programs through their observatories or at meeting places. You can hear a talk about astronomy and look through telescopes, guided by volunteers.

■ Dress warmly. Even summer nights in the country can get quite cool.

■ Bring insect repellent during warm weather.

■ Take a comfortable outdoor chair so you can appreciate the sky longer.

■ Choose a safe location — and do not trespass.

■ Don't forget to bring the kids!

— *Vic and Jen Winter*

Future total solar eclipses through the United States

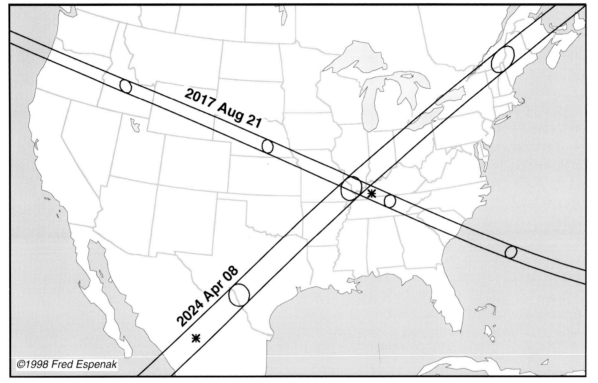

Illustration courtesy of Fred Espenak, NASA

During the first quarter of the 21st century, only two total eclipses of the sun will be visible from the continental United States. They occur on Aug. 21, 2017 and April 8, 2024.

Gary Lezak

Chief meteorologist at KSHB-TV, the NBC affiliate in Kansas City, Gary has been fascinated by weather phenomena for as long as he can remember. While Gary was growing up in southern California, his idol and inspiration was George Fishbeck, a weathercaster in Los Angeles.

Knowing the weather was more exciting in other parts of the country, Gary enrolled at the University of Oklahoma, where he received a bachelor of science in meteorology in 1985. He began a broadcasting career that brought him to Kansas City in 1992.

Gary won the Kansas City Media Professionals award for Television Reporter-Sports/Weather in 1997 and 1998. He also won awards for best weather graphics and overall show at weather seminars in 1994, 1997, and 2001. He won the Missouri Broadcasters Association award for Best Weathercast in 2000. Gary has the American Meteorology Society seal of approval for television broadcasting.

He takes his dogs, Windy and Stormy, to about 70 public appearances a year. There he helps students and adults learn how the weather works. Although Gary's favorite subjects are cloud types and precipitation, he spends most of the time on tornadoes and tornado safety. Windy and Stormy appear at the end of his presentations to perform for the audience.

Gary also enjoys working out, participates in many sports activities and is an avid sports fan. First and foremost, however, is his hobby: Watching the weather.

He can be reached by email at lezak@kshb.com.

Vic and Jen Winter

"At a very young age I was permitted to stay up late and watch something amazing in the sky above," Vic recalls. "A bright, shiny, star-like object passed overhead as twilight faded. I witnessed Sputnik and the start of space race.

"A few years passed and I was still looking up. I thrilled watching man take his first steps on the moon on a tiny black-and-white television, then stepped outside and looked up at the real thing. The small telescope I owned at that time was the next best thing to being there."

Vic Winter was born in Kansas and has lived in the Midwest most of his adult life. He began his photographic career in the 1960s and won a photography award from the William Randolph Hearst Foundation when he was at Kansas State University in the 1970s. His career took him to Bartlesville, Okla., and eventually to *The Kansas City Star*. In 1980 he was honored as the National Press Photographers Association's Photographer of the Year for the Midwest.

Vic has been involved in amateur astronomy since the middle 1980s and has been president of the Astronomical Society of Kansas City as well as director of the society's observatory. Vic also holds seven major observing awards from the Astronomical League and was voted regional amateur astronomer of the year in 1987.

Today, Vic and Jen own and operate www.ICSTARS.com, an educational astronomy website where visitors can look at their photographs and learn about the sky. The couple's photographs have been published in magazines, books and on internet sites worldwide. They travel around the world capturing astronomical events such as total eclipses in Africa and southern hemisphere delights in Bolivia. They lead

others on these expeditions through their travel company, Astronomical Tours.

In 1999 they founded the StarGarden Foundation, a not-for-profit organization dedicated to the advancement of astronomy education in the Kansas City area. The two also are editors of The Reflector, the national quarterly publication of the Astronomical League.

Vic and Jen can be reached by email at webmaster@ICSTARS.com.

PHOTO CREDITS

All photographs are by Vic and Jen Winter unless noted. For astronomical photographs the object, time, place and equipment used are listed.

Dust jacket/cover. Star trails, Feb. 10, 2002, Johnson County, Missouri. Neighbor Mike Riggs' tractor is framed by the streaks of stars rotating around the north pole in this four-hour exposure using a Nikon F2 with 20mm lens, tripod-mounted.

i. Aurora, March 31st, 2001, Johnson County, Kansas. Nikon N90s with 50mm lens, 30-second exposure on a tripod.

ii. Comet Hale-Bopp, March 16, 1997, Powell Botanical Gardens Chapel, Johnson County, Missouri. Nikon F3 with 85mm lens. Ten-minute guided exposure highlighted with headlights.

iv. Milky Way, June 1999. Composite of four images, each a 10-minute guided exposures on a motorized LosMandy GM-8 telescope mount with a Nikon 50mm lens at f2.8.

vi. Gary Lezak.

4-5. Sunrise, September 2000, Linn County, Kansas. Nikon N90s with 80-200mm lens.

7. Dawn, Sept. 3, 1988, Linn County, Kansas. Nikon F3 with 180mm lens.

8. Mare's tails, Nov. 19, 1990, Johnson County, Kansas. Nikon F3 with 80-200 lens.

9. Cloud edge, November 1994, Jefferson County, Colorado. Nikon F4 with 80-200mm lens.

10-11. Silver lining, July 4, 1995, Miami County, Kansas. Nikon F4 with 80-200mm lens.

12-13. Gary Lezak photos.

16. Prominence arch, April 15, 2001, Johnson County, Kansas. Special solar telescope with SI Systems Hydrogen Alpha filter. Nikon F2 with 5,000mm telescope.

17. Sun halo, May 26, 1990, Prude Ranch, Jeff Davis County, Texas. Nikon F3 with 20mm lens.

18-19. Boiling sun, Oct. 20, 2000, Johnson County, Kansas. Special solar telescope with SI Systems .4 angstrom Hydrogen Alpha filter. Nikon F2 with 5,000mm telescope.

20-21. Big bite eclipse, Dec. 14, 2001. Unfiltered 600mm telephoto lens near sunset with Nikon N90s.

21. Christmas eclipse, Dec. 25, 2000. Nikon N90s with 600mm telephoto lens and white light solar.

22. Diamond ring, August 1999, Lake Hazar, Turkey. 500mm telescope with no filter on a guided telescope mount.

23. Totality, June 2001, Morombe, Madagascar. Composite of 13 separate images taken during totality combined using Adobe Photoshop. Five-inch f8 telescope with a 2x barlow and no filter. Exposures vary from 4 seconds to 1/250th of a second.

24-25. Sun dog, Nov. 19, 1990, Johnson County, Kansas. Nikon F3 with 80-200 lens.

29. Thunderheads, July 1989, Miami County, Kansas. Nikon F3 with 180mm lens.

30, 31. Fields and storm, July 4, 1995, Miami County, Kansas. Nikon F4 with 20mm lens.

32-33. Western Kansas storm, Aug. 9, 2000, Stanton County, Kansas. Nikon N90s with 80-200mm lens.

34-35. Mammatus clouds, June 13, 1998, Clay County, Missouri. Nikon N90s with 80-200mm lens.

35. Shelf cloud, June 1986, Neosho County, Kansas. Canon AE-1 with 50mm lens.

36-37. Lightning, June 28, 1976, Tuttle Creek Lake, Riley County, Kansas. Multiple exposures. Nikon F2 with 105mm lens.

37. Plains lightning, August 1992, Linn County, Kansas. Two-minute exposure, tripod mount, Nikon F2 with 20mm lens.

38-39. Tornado, spring 1980, Labette County, Kansas. Nikon F2 with 85mm lens.

40. Puddle jumper, April 19, 1981, Osage County, Oklahoma. Jason Shambles, (age 10 at the time) pauses with his dogs amid the puddles after an Oklahoma thunderstorm.

41. Double rainbow, Aug. 19, 1987, Johnson County, Kansas. Nikon F3 with 24mm lens.

42-43. Rainy rainbow, Sept. 30, 2000, Linn County, Kansas. Nikon N90s with 20mm lens.

44. Barn Rainbow, Sept. 30, 2000, Linn County, Kansas. Nikon N90s with 20mm lens.

45. Sun shaft, August 1985, Colorado. Nikon F2 and 105mm lens.

46-47. Sunset shaft and barn, June 14, 1991, Linn County, Kansas. Nikon F3 with 180mm lens.

52. Sunset tree, April 9, 1990, Linn County, Kansas. Nikon F3 with 300mm lens.

53. Sunset contrails, Sept. 29, 2000, Linn County, Kansas. Nikon N90s with a 20mm lens.

54. Cloud shadows, Aug. 7, 2002, Colorado. Nikon N90s with 80-200mm lens.

55. Stormy sunset, Sept. 30, 2000, Linn County, Kansas. Nikon N90s with a 20mm lens.

56-57. Jupiter-Mercury sunset, May 5, 1989, Linn County, Kansas. Nikon F2 with 50mm lens.

61. Big and Little Dippers, Feb. 16, 2002, Johnson County, Missouri. Mamiya 645J with 80mm lens, mounted on motorized telescope mount. Two guided exposures of 20 minutes each combined using Adobe Photoshop.

62. Star trails, August 1995, Cherry County, Nebraska. Nikon F4 with 20mm lens. Two-hour exposure on a tripod.

63. Orion region, Dec. 4, 1986, Miami County, Kansas. Ten-minute guided exposure, Nikon F2 with 50mm lens, mounted on motorized Celestron C-8 telescope.

64. The Pleiades, Dec. 4, 1986, Miami County, Kansas. Fifteen-minute guided exposure, Nikon F2 with 180mm lens, mounted on motorized Celestron C-8 telescope.

65. Farm light fog, Sept. 20, 2001, Johnson County, Missouri. Thirty-second exposure, Mamiya 645J with 80mm lens, tripod-mounted.

66-67. Summer Milky Way, August 1993. Composite of four 10-minute exposures using a Nikon 50mm lens guided by a motorized Meade 10-inch telescope.

68. Great Orion nebula, December 1989, Miami County, Kansas. Eight-minute guided exposure using a 29-inch telescope and Nikon F2.

69. Antares region, June 1999, Miami County, Kansas. Two 35-minute exposures combined using a Nikon F2 with 85mm lens, guided by a motorized LosMandy GM-8 telescope mount.

70. Hale-Bopp, March 20, 1997, Jackson County, Missouri. Nikon F2 with a 180mm lens, mounted on a Meade 10 inch motorized telescope. A guided 6 minute exposure.

74. Hale-Bopp over pond, March 26, 1997, Washington County, Oklahoma. Thirty-second exposure using a Nikon F2 with 50mm lens, tripod-mounted.

75. Hale-Bopp over the Country Club Plaza, March 30, 1997, Jackson County, Missouri. Twenty-second exposure, Nikon F2 with 180mm lens, tripod-mounted.

76. Hyakutake, Venus and pond, April 9, 1996, Johnson County, Missouri. Five-minute exposure, Nikon F2 with 20mm lens, tripod-mounted.

77. Hyakutake and dome, March 26, 1996, Johnson County, Missouri. Five-minute exposure, Nikon F2 with 20mm lens, tripod-mounted.

78-79. Leonid meteor storm, Nov. 18, 2001. More than 150 meteors can be seen streaking from the meteor shower radiant in the constellation of Leo in this composite of more than 20 photographs. Ten-minute exposures, four Nikon cameras with 50mm lens, all on LosMandy GM-8 motorized mount.

80. Leonid bolide, Nov. 17, 1998, Miami County, Kansas. A huge Bolide or fireball can be seen in this "all-sky" photograph, a composite of 11 separate negatives, each exposed 15 minutes. Nikon F2 with 8mm fisheye lens, tripod-mounted and pointed straight up.

81. Leonid face, Nov. 17, 1998, Miami County, Kansas. The train left by a fireball meteor forms a curious shape in the night sky. Fifteen-minute exposure, Nikon F2 with 8mm fisheye lens, tripod-mounted and pointed straight up.

82. Space shuttle and Perseids, Aug. 11, 1998, Johnson

County, Missouri. Fifteen-minute exposure, Nikon F2 with 16mm lens, tripod mounted.

83. Iridium Flare, Aug. 11, 2001, Johnson County, Missouri. Nikon F2 with a 50mm lens and 10 minute exposure mounted on a LosMandy GM-8 motorized mount.

84-85. Totality prominences, June 21, 2001. Huge solar prominences can be seen in this unfiltered photograph of the sun's limb using a 5-inch f8 Hruska telescope with a 4x barlow lens mounted on a LosMandy GM-8 motorized mount.

85. Active region, March 29, 2001. Nikon F2 using a 5,000mm special solar telescope with SI Systems .4 angstrom Hydrogen Alpha filter.

85. Aurora, March 31, 2001, Johnson County, Kansas. Thirty-second exposure, Nikon N90s with 35mm lens, tripod-mounted.

86-87. Powell Observatory aurora, Nov. 8, 1991. Miami County, Kansas. Thirty-second exposure, Nikon F2 with 24mm lens, tripod-mounted.

89. Moon, Aug. 26, 1983, Washington County, Oklahoma. Nikon F2 at prime focus with a Celestron C-8 motorized telescope.

90. Moon and airplane, September 1989, Johnson County, Kansas. Nikon F3 with 400mm lens.

91. Moon, top photo: September 1993. Bottom photo: August 1993, Miami County Kansas. Nikon F2 mounted at prime focus on a Meade 10-inch motorized telescope.

92. Red eclipse, April 3, 1996, Miami County Kansas. NikonF2 with 400mm lens, tripod-mounted.

93. Total lunar eclipse, Jan. 20, 2000, Jackson County, Missouri. Five-second exposure, Nikon N90s at prime focus on a Celestron C-5 telescope guided on a LosMandy GM-8

94. Moon ring, Jan. 27, 2002, Johnson County, Kansas. Ten-second exposure, Nikon N90s with 20mm lens, tripod-mounted.

95. Moon penumbra, Jan. 20, 2000, Jackson County, Missouri. Nikon N90s with 80-200 lens.

96. K-Hill under full moon, Oct. 17, 1986, Riley County, Kansas. Nikon F3 with 600mm telephoto lens, tripod-mounted.

97. Jupiter occultation, Sept 15, 1990, Linn County, Kansas. Twenty-second guided exposure, Nikon F2 at prime focus of 12.2-inch reflector telescope.

98-99. Saturn occultation, Dec. 28, 2001, Johnson County, Missouri. Nikon F2 at prime focus of a 9.25 inch Celestron telescope with a 4x barlow lens for a 9,400mm focal length.

100. Moon/Jupiter/Venus, April 23, 1998, Jackson County, Missouri. Twenty-second exposure, Nikon N90s with 180mm lens, tripod-mounted.

102. Mercury transit, Nov. 15, 1999, Miami County Kansas.

Special solar telescope (5,000mm) with SI Systems .2 angstrom Hydrogen Alpha filter. Multiple 1/60-second exposures with Nikon F2. Composite made with Adobe Photoshop.

103. Mars/Lagoon/Trifid, May 24, 2001. Greatly overexposed planet Mars passes by the Lagoon and Trifid nebulas with a Mamiya 645J at prime focus on a 5-inch refractor. Thirty-minute guided exposure mounted on a LosMandy GM-8 motorized mount.

104. Mars, Oct. 19, 1988, Powell Observatory, Miami County Kansas. One-quarter-second exposure, NikonF2 with eyepiece projection at prime focus of 29-inch telescope.

104-105. Moon and Venus, Sept. 29, 2000, Linn County, Kansas. Twenty-second exposure, Nikon N90s with 80-200mm lens, tripod-mounted.

106. Venus, Dec. 27, 1989, Miami County, Kansas. One-eighth-second exposure. Nikon F2 with eyepiece projection at prime focus of 29-inch telescope.

107. Moon/Venus/Jupiter, Sept 15, 1990, Linn County, Kansas. Twenty-second exposure, Nikon F3 with 85mm lens, tripod-mounted.

108. Crepuscular rays, April 26, 1998, Johnson County, Missouri. Nikon N90s with 80-200mm lens.

110. Comet Hyakutake. March 21, 1996, Elmcrest Observatory, Powell Botanical Gardens, Johnson County, Missouri, 15-minute exposure, 200mm lens, Nikon F2 mounted on a Meade 10-inch motorized telescope.

112. Clouds, July 1980, Washington County, Oklahoma. Nikon F2 with 50mm lens.

114, 115. Dave Eames, *The Star.*

117. Courtesy Fred Espenak.

118. Gary Lezak.

119. File photo, *The Star.*

122. Crepuscular rays, Sept., 2001, Miami County, Kansas, Nikon 90s with 20mm lens.

SOURCES OF QUOTATIONS

■ Louis F. Burns. *Osage Indian Customs and Myths.* Fallbrook, Calif.: Ciga Press. 1984.

■ William E.Connelley, ed. *The Journals of William Walker, Provisional Governor of Nebraska Territory.* Lincoln, Neb.: State Journal Co. 1899.

■ Gottfried Duden. *Gottfried Duden's "Report (on a Journey to the Western States),"* 1824-1827 translated by William G. Bek. 1919.

■ Drumm, Stella M., ed. Down the Santa Fe Trail and Into Mexico: The Diary of Susan Shelby Magoffin, 1846-1847. Lincoln: University of Nebraska Press, 1982.

■ Max Greene. *The Kanzas Region: Forest, Prairie, Desert, Mountain, Vale, and River....* New York: Fowler and Wells, Publishers. 1856.

■ Josiah Gregg. *Commerce of the Prairies* (Max Moorhead, ed.) Norman, Okla.: University of Oklahoma Press, 1954.

■ *History of St. Charles, Montgomery, and Warren counties, Missouri....* St. Louis: National Historical Co., 1885.

■ William E. Koch. *Folklore from Kansas: Customs, Beliefs, and Superstitions.* Lawrence, Kan.: Regents Press of Kansas. 1980.

■ *Land of Enchantment: Memoirs of Marian Russell Along the Santa Fe Trail as Dictated to Mrs. Hall Russell.* Albuquerque, N.M. University of New Mexico Press. 1954.

■ Randolph B. Marcy. *The Prairie Traveler. A Hand-book for Overland Expeditions....* Washington: United States War Department. 1859

■ Alice Marriott and Carol K. Rachlin. *Plains Indian Mythology.* New York: Thomas Y. Crowell Co. 1975.

■ James F. Meline. *Two Thousand Miles on Horseback. Santa Fe and Back. A Summer Tour Through Kansas, Nebraska, Colorado and New Mexico, in the Year 1866.* New York: Hurd and Houghton. 1868.

■ Francis Parkman. (E.N. Feltskog, ed.) *The Oregon Trail.* Madison, Wis.: The University of Wisconsin Press. 1969.

■ William Sheehan and Stephen James O'Meara. *Mars: The Lure of the Red Planet.* Amherst, N.Y.: Prometheus Books.

Miami County, Kansas